SPOTLIGHT ON

Romantic Style

Five Original Pieces for the Intermediate Pianist
in Preparation for the Works of Chopin

CATHERINE ROLLIN

FOREWORD

As a piano teacher, I always look forward to the point in my students' development when they can begin to play the Romantic masterworks, particularly those of Chopin. For most of these works, however, students must have reached at least an early advanced level.

In *Spotlight on Romantic Style*, I have tried to create pieces that capture the most important elements of the Romantic era: expressive, cantabile melodies and full-bodied sound. These pieces, however, stay firmly within the reach of the intermediate student. Each piece explores a different form. Through this collection, students and teachers are offered a fulfilling musical experience while preparing for the Romantic masterworks.

CONTENTS

Alfred

Nocturne

Andante cantabile

Catherine Rollin

13
mp
cresc.
dim.
16
a tempo – poco più mosso
poco rit.
mp
19
mf
cresc.
22
f
rit.
dim.
p

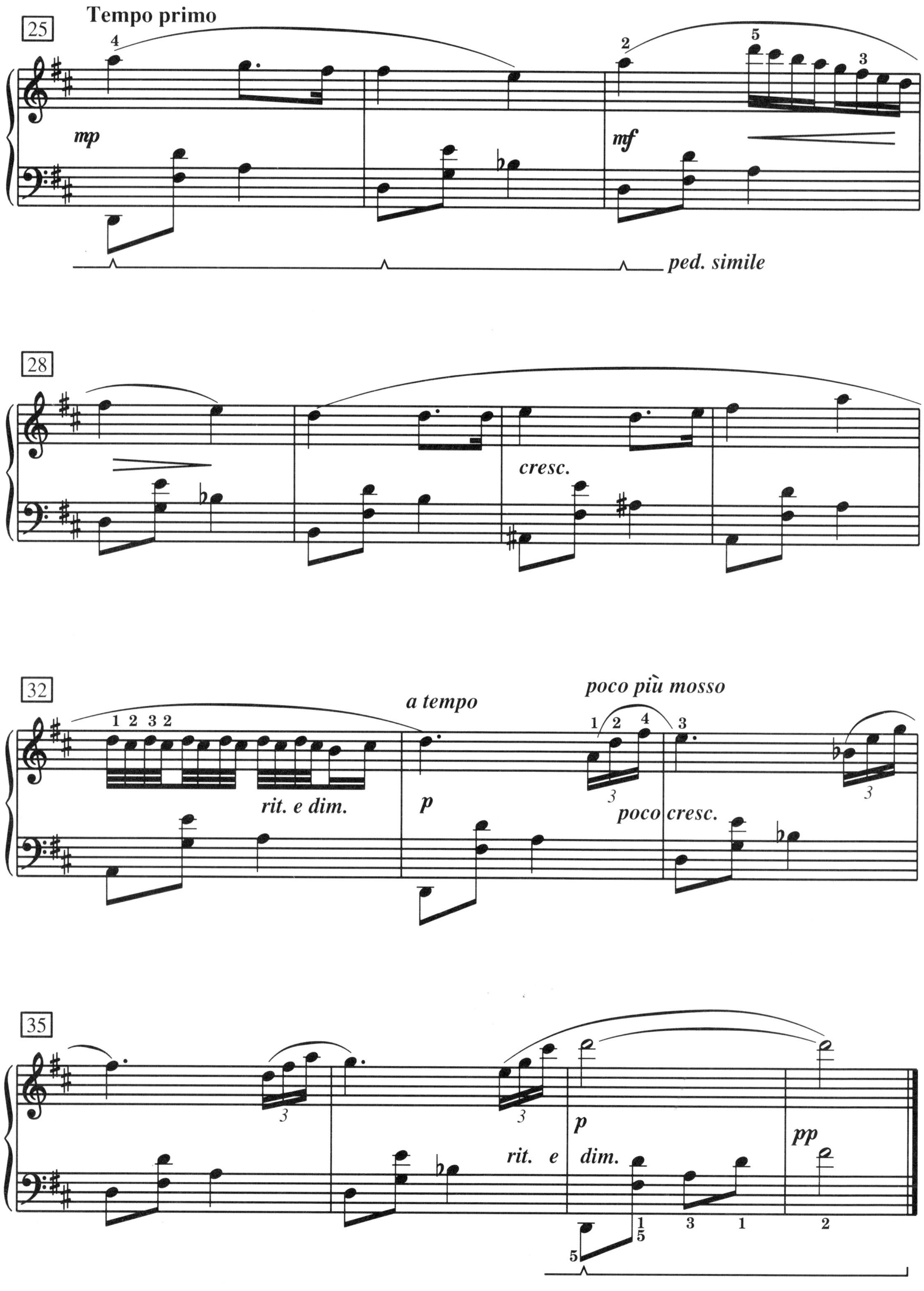
25
Tempo primo
mp
mf
ped. simile
28
cresc.
32
rit. e dim.
a tempo
poco più mosso
p
poco cresc.
35
rit. e dim.
p
pp

Waltz

Allegretto
espressivo

Catherine Rollin

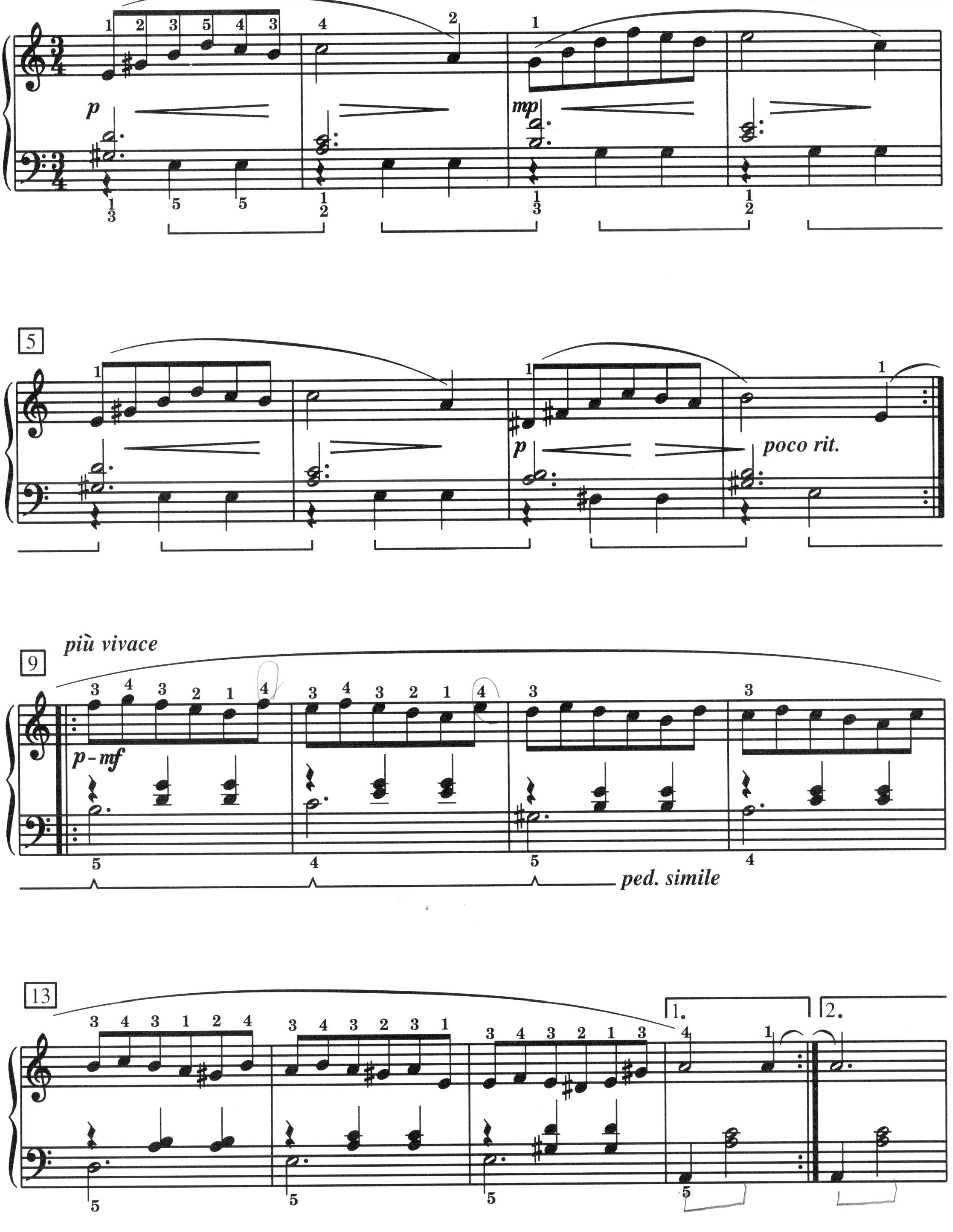

18 Tempo primo
mp
mf
21
24
p
poco rit.
più vivace
3 4 3 2 1 4
mp - mf
27
ped. simile

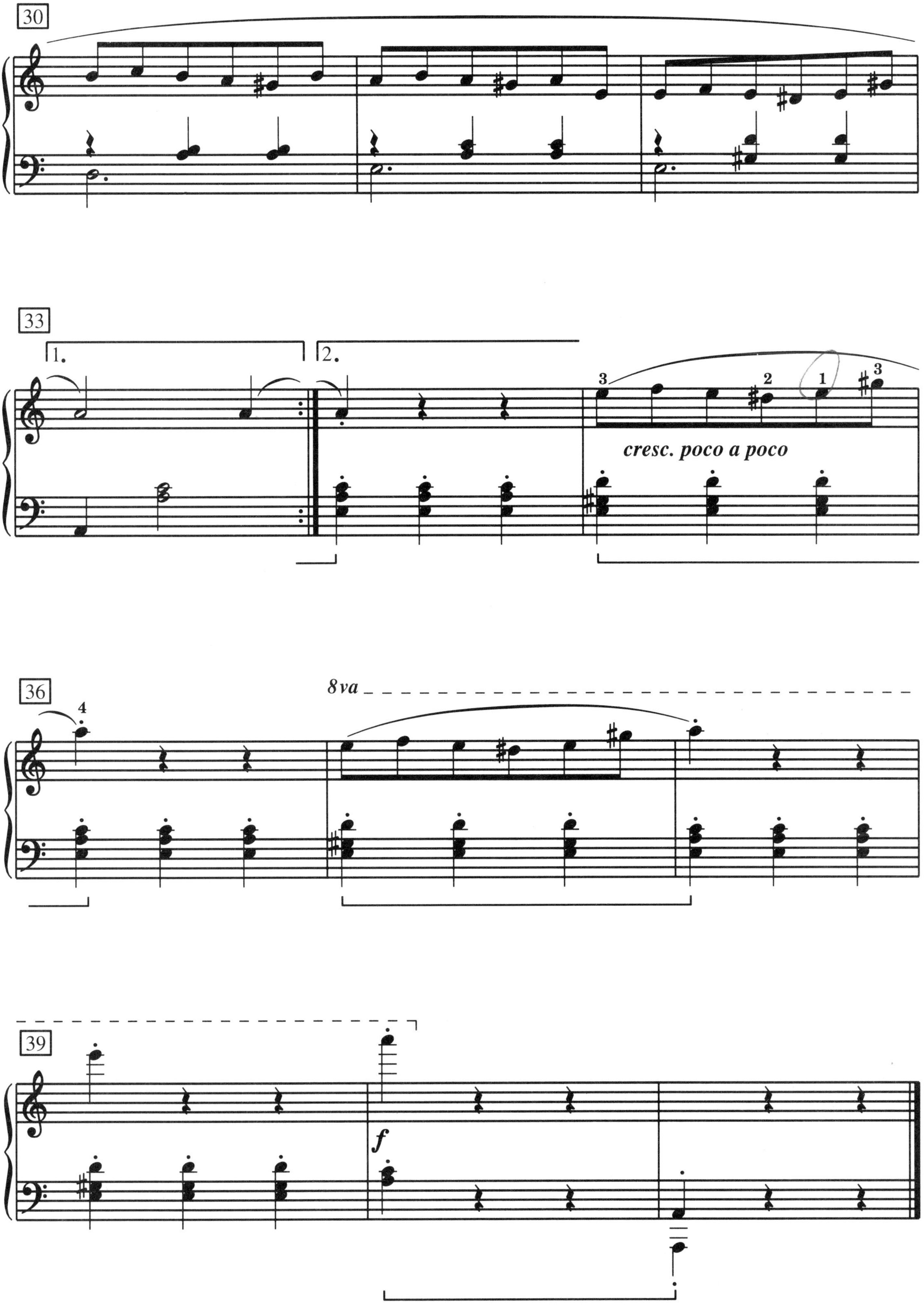
30
33
1.
2.
cresc. poco a poco
36
8va
39
f

Mazurka

Moderato animato

Catherine Rollin

cresc.
dim.

30
mp
cresc.
mf
35
dim.
p
cresc.
40
mp
dim.
p
45
a tempo
mp
poco rit.
p

Polonaise

Catherine Rollin

13
mf
f
16
poco rit. e dim.
a tempo
mf
19
mp
22
to Coda
poco rit.

25
a tempo
p
mp
28
mf
f
31
D.S. al Coda
mf
rit.
CODA
34
p
mp
dim. e rit.
p

Etude

Catherine Rollin

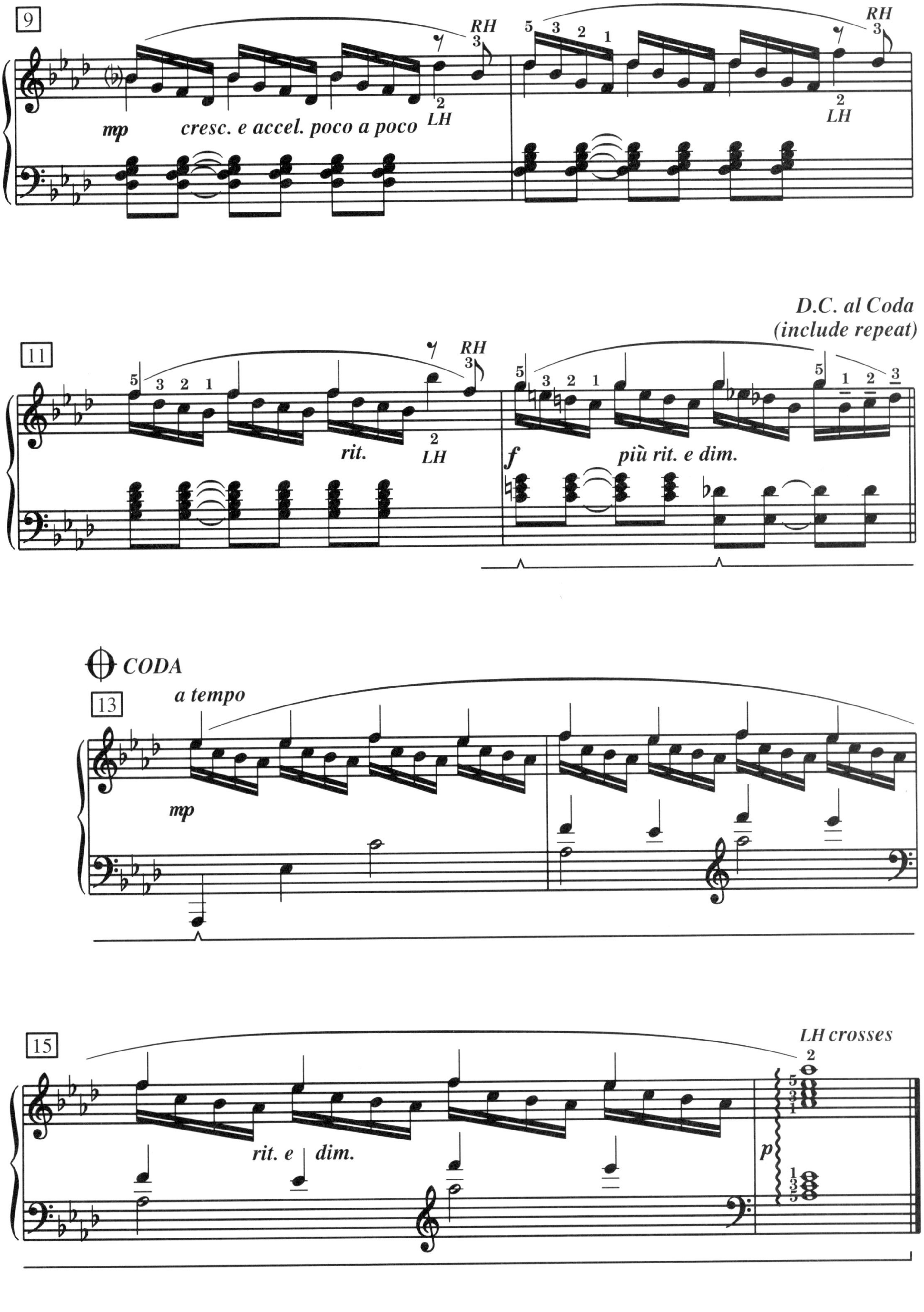
9
mp
cresc. e accel. poco a poco
RH
LH
11
rit.
D.C. al Coda
(include repeat)
f
più rit. e dim.
CODA
13
a tempo
mp
15
rit. e
dim.
LH crosses
p

Suggestions & Program Notes

ETUDE is a study that emphasizes a particular technical point. The etudes of Chopin created a new genre, the concert etude. These were studies that (from a musical standpoint) could also be performed publicly. This etude is intended to develop the ability to voice with the fifth finger of the right hand. An effective practice method would be to play the inner 16th notes staccato while holding each quarter note with the fifth finger. This will help lighten the touch on the inside of the hand. In keeping with the Romantic tradition, this etude is also intended for public performance. *(pg. 14)*

MAZURKA is a Polish folk dance in 3/4 meter that tends to stress the weak beat. In this mazurka, the accentuation is generally on beat two. It is important to follow the pedaling and the articulation so this aspect of the mazurka is captured. The melodic material is simple and attempts to reflect the folk quality that infused the original mazurkas with their special spirit. *(pg. 8)*

NOCTURNE, meaning "night song," was a form developed by the Irish keyboard composer John Field. The form was then brought to its greatest heights by Frédéric Chopin, who explored intimate emotions through beautiful, cantabile melodies that were often highly ornamented. In this nocturne, the ornaments are already realized in the score. The primary emphasis should be on beautiful tone and legato playing. *(pg. 2)*

POLONAISE is a Polish national dance also in 3/4 meter. It has a stately quality derived largely from the repeated  pattern that is characteristic of the Romantic-style polonaise. In this polonaise, that particular pattern is in the left hand, contrasted with a broad melody in the right hand throughout most of the piece. *(pg. 11)*

WALTZ is a dance in triple meter with the emphasis on the downbeat. Beats two and three should always be played very lightly in the left hand for an effective waltz feel. During the Romantic period, the waltz developed into elegant art music characterized by grace and often a bit of flamboyance. The waltz herein has a simple melody in the **A** section with a trace of melancholy. The **B** section should be played with flair, which can be easily achieved by observing the correct fingering. *(pg. 5)*